Selected Verse
of
THOMAS D'ARCY McGEE

Selected Verse
of
THOMAS D'ARCY McGEE

Edited with an Introduction by
SEÁN VIRGO

TORONTO
Exile Editions
1991

Copyright © Exile Editions, 1991

This Edition is published by Exile Editions Ltd.,
20 Dale Avenue, Toronto, Ontario, Canada M4W 1K4

Sales Distribution
General Publishing Co. Ltd.
30 Lesmill Road, Don Mills, Ontario M3B 2T6

Designed by LOU LUCIANI
Typeset in STEMPEL *by* TUMAX
Printed in Canada by UNIVERSITY OF TORONTO PRESS

ISBN 1-5509-6012-1

The publisher wishes to acknowledge the assistance towards publication of the Canada Council and the Ontario Arts Council

—

PREFACE

1985 was the year of the "Shamrock Summit." Two men whom I regard as scoundrels held hands on the Plains of Abraham and sang "*When Irish Eyes Are Smiling.*" Now that is one of those mawkish ditties, usually written by Englishmen, which romanticise the safely marginalised Celt. "In the sound of Irish laughter" I do not "hear the angels sing" – Yeats' "Porter drinkers' randy laughter" is more to my taste, and closer to the truth. The song those men were singing is remembered by most Irishmen as what Billy Conn would bawl out in the ring after he had pummelled the bejesus out of some hapless opponent. The brutal falsity of the words was perfect for that.

The two men sang, and our country slipped towards Free Trade, towards "bottom line" politics, towards the unkind '80s, the neglect of our educational system and our artists, towards our jackalhood in the Persian Gulf.

D'Arcy McGee died for Canada. "Great the treasures that you guard Along the line! Along the line!" he wrote, and "the line" for him was not just the U.S. border, but a whole division of values.

He must have turned in his grave.

It was at about that time that my publisher, Barry Callaghan, suggested that I might look through McGee's 1869 *Collected Poems*. McGee was much better, he thought, than most people realized: the anthologies had got him wrong. Barry was right.

We live in dark times but we are still more fortunate than most. McGee's poems delight and surprise, but they remind us too that Canada was founded on a distinctive vision of justice and equality. I habitually separate poetry from politics, but in McGee's case that is not always possible. He was called "Friend of the Poor," and his sense of poverty had as much to do with ignorance as with economics.

We should attend, again, to his message.

KINLOUGH, ONTARIO. 1991.

CONTENTS

INTRODUCTION / ix
IMPROMPTU / 3
MIDSUMMER, 1851 / 4
A MALEDICTION / 6
SONG OF THE SURPLUS / 7
THE EXILE'S MEDITATION / 8
DEEDS DONE IN DAYS OF SHAME / 9
"WHEN FIGHTING WAS THE FASHION" / 10
THE READER'S SONG / 11
THE EXILE'S DEVOTION / 13
THE HEART'S RESTING-PLACE / 15
EXECUTION OF ARCHBISHOP PLUNKETT / 16
THE THREE MINSTRELS / 17
LORD GL—GALL'S DREAM / 19
THE MAN OF THE NORTH COUNTRIE / 21
THE CELT'S PRAYER / 22
THE TRIP OVER THE MOUNTAIN / 23
THE PRAYER TO ST. BRENDAN / 25
AN INVITATION WESTWARD / 26
IT IS EASY TO DIE / 27
TO MY WISHING-CAP / 28
SONNET – RETURN / 29
THE IRISH HOMES OF ILLINOIS / 30
THE SHANTY / 31
"THE ARMY OF THE WEST" / 33
A SALUTATION TO THE FREE FLAG OF AMERICA / 34
FREEDOM'S JOURNEY / 35
ALONG THE LINE / 36
ICEBERGS / 37
THE DEATH OF HUDSON / 38
THE LAUNCH OF THE GRIFFIN / 43
"OUR LADYE OF THE SNOW!" / 46

JACQUES CARTIER / 51
JACQUES CARTIER AND THE CHILD / 53
THE ARCTIC INDIAN'S FAITH / 54
PEACE HATH HER VICTORIES / 55
A PLEA FOR THE POOR / 56
RICH AND POOR / 57
FALSE FEAR OF THE WORLD / 59
GRANDMA ALICE / 60
AUTUMN AND WINTER / 62
THE MOUNTAIN-LAUREL / 63
THE DEATH-BED / 64
DARK BLUE EYES / 66
A CONTRAST / 67
TO MARY'S ANGEL / 68
CONSOLATION / 69
A SMALL CATECHISM / 70
GOD BE PRAISED / 71
CHRISTMAS MORN / 73
THE MIDNIGHT MASS / 74
LIFE, A MYSTERY TO MAN / 76
ACKNOWLEDGEMENT / 80

INTRODUCTION

His last words were "God bless you."

The House had sat well past midnight. The parliament of the new Dominion was closing its first session. Thomas D'Arcy McGee, Independent, member for Montreal West, former minister of Agriculture and Immigration, had spoken at length of Canada's challenges and destiny. His subject was Confederation, signed less than a year before and still distrusted by the Maritime provinces. He had been its chief prophet, and one of the signing Fathers.

> "Its single aim," he concluded, "from the beginning has been to consolidate the extent of British North America with the utmost regard to the independent power and privileges of each province and I, Sir, who have been and still am its warm and earnest advocate speak here not as the representative of any race, or of any province, but as thoroughly and emphatically a Canadian, ready and bound to recognise the claims of my Canadian fellow subjects from the furthest east to the furthest west, equally as those of my nearest neighbour or the friend who proposed me on the hustlings."

We must take on trust his contemporaries' descriptions of his voice, as we must take on trust descriptions of Garrick or Keane. Assuming the "high, firm, silvery tenor" which helped make him the most famous and best-paid public speaker of his day, the words in themselves keep their resonance now, 113 years later. The ironies in that resonance I need hardly point out.

The sitting ended in a rare mood of bonhomie. Freed for the first time from party allegiances and antagonisms, McGee's eloquence had flowed with none of the contentious wit and *ad hominem* riposte for which he was renowned and feared. There was a magnanimity at play here, too: he was, in effect, a has-been. "C'est certain," the Conservative *La Minerve* had crowed in September, "que M. McGee est 'a dead duck.'" Political expediency, the juggling of French and Irish votes, of Quebec and Maritime representation, had seen him left out of the first Canadian cabinet; and Sir John A. MacDonald was grateful for (and relieved at) the grace with which he had withdrawn. His impassioned war against Fenianism (which would cost him his life within the hour) had lost him so much support in his own constituency that he had barely been re-elected; and politicians have their own bemused fondness for men whose principles outweigh self-interest. They cheered him to the rafters.

He left the House with his young friend, Robert McFarlane, in the quiet, satisfied glow of a man at the end of a career in politics, respected by friend and adversary alike, still able to hold the House in thrall to his oratory. They strolled through the deserted streets of the country's young capital, their cigar smoke lingering on the frosty, spring-tinged air.

They passed the site of today's Canada Council headquarters and, at the corner of Metcalfe and Sparks Streets, McGee turned off towards his lodgings. "Good-night," said McFarlane. "God bless you," McGee called back, reaching into his pocket for his front door key. The next thing McFarlane heard was a pistol shot.

The man who fired the shot had been waiting for hours, alone with himself in a doorway, hearing the distant rush of the Chaudiere Falls, watching the houseshadows sweep across Sparks Street as the moon climbed through the April night. He would have heard the young pages dashing home from the House and known that the time was near. Would have seen the two men pause at the mouth of the street and heard the "Goodnight" and "God bless you." And known his man.

McGee came slowly, a short figure in a dark overcoat, his pale hat picked out by the moonlight. His face was obscured, but the cane and the careful, limping gait identified him. But how much is a man a man in the eyes of his assassin? He is a target, an object focussed by hate and self-righteousness. The assassin's heartbeat, the silver of adrenalin in his gums, the barely controllable tremor in his knee were more human at that moment than the figure which stopped on the sidewalk, ground out its cigar, switched its cane to its left arm and mounted the house steps.

As it reached with its latchkey towards the door, the assassin stepped forward and thrust his revolver under the hat brim. At that moment the door opened inward. The assassin fired, and ran.

Was it James Patrick Whelan, condemned on good evidence and hanged two months later? He protested his innocence to the gallows and there's no way for history to know if he fired the revolver. His confessor knew (for McGee lived, wrote and died in a Catholic world) and it's strange that a shriven man would go out on a lie, when he could have claimed a defiant, Fenian heroism. His confessor knew, and could only speak to God. If Whelan was innocent, then others knew, and let him die and held their tongues to the grave.

The woman who opened the door on the murder was not looking for Mr McGee. Mrs Trotter, the boarding house owner, was waiting for Will, her 13 year old son, a page at the House not yet allowed his own latchkey. She saw the pistol's flash. McGee dropped to his knees, struggled briefly to rise, and fell back down the steps. Just a moment later young Will was there, staring up at his mother across the body.

The boy did not speak. He raced on down the street to the *Times* office, where the lights still burned, and burst in upon the compositors: "Mr McGee has been shot!"

The printers and editors came out into Sparks Street. They joined the small crowd, most of them from the House, who were gathering round the body. McGee's cane was still hooked on his left arm, his hat just slightly down over his eyes. A puddle of blood spread out from his mouth across the sidewalk; the rattle of death was audible.

Sir John A. Macdonald was one of the crowd. He was one of those who knelt, lifted McGee from the sidewalk and carried him into the parlour.

The first pallbearers, then, were politicians and newspapermen. It was fitting enough, for McGee had been both most of his adult life. If history were neat in its ironies, though, there would have been a poet there too.

For at this point D'Arcy McGee enters a safe and unenviable niche in our consciousness, as one of the handful of Canadians who are remembered for their violent deaths. Brébeuf, Riel, Almighty Voice, Charcoal, the Donnelleys, the Mad Trapper: these form the *grand guignol* of popular history, a marginal glamour upon our meagre past, to be co-opted in each generation by provincial novelists and playwrights, or resurrected for tourist pageants.

But the Fenian bullet cut off another career than politics. And passionate as McGee was in all his causes, quixotic and impulsive in his life, controversial and combative in three countries, his main sense of himself was as a poet: first as inheritor of the Irish bardic mantle ("Harp of the land I love! forgive this hand/That reverently lifts thee from the dust"), and later as the founding father of a Canadian literature ("the existence of a recognised literary class will by and by be felt as a state and social necessity").

His friends and colleagues understood this priority. Though McGee fretted about his survival after politics, and muttered against "those infernal gods, the publishers," the grateful Macdonald had offered him a sinecure. As Commissioner of Patents, McGee was to be paid nearly $3500 a year (a cabinet salary was about $4000) and since he could command up to $250 for a public lecture, he could look forward to a comfortable enough life as a poet.

He was a week short of his 43rd birthday when he died.

He sits apart, hunched in a chair in Robert Harris' "*Fathers of Confederation,*" like a man half-attending to a sermon. He seems to be dwarfed by Charles Tupper, the speaking figure who stands in front of him and receives the full attention of Sir John A., but in fact McGee's blocking (*downstage left, seated*) is one that any actor would recognise and covet. It is a classic upstaging ploy, always in focus (for our western eyes read pictures and stages, like books, from left to right) and implying both silent, ironic commentary and impending action. Something about him appealed, evidently, to the painter's eye.

He holds a folio on his knee. He is less comfortable in his dress-clothes than anyone else in the chamber, and his face comes close to conventional English caricatures of the Paddy. The long upper lip, the coarse features, the rug-headed brow and, compounding these, a more than swarthy complexion. This was "Darky McGee," proposed by Uncle Tom, proprietor of his favourite bar, the Cabin, as "Negro candidate for the next election."

Ours is a cynical age, a reductive, muckraking age with contempt above all for our own choice of leaders. Our sense of honour is Falstaff's, not Hotspur's, and our distrust of idealism – its power and hypocrisy – is what marks us out most, perhaps, from Americans. And it is true that the ideal of Liberty which led McGee first to rebellion and then to the New World, is as likely to lead to Jacobin Paris, the napalming of Vietnam's forests, the arming of Contra guerrillas or the saturation bombing of shell-shocked Iraqui conscripts, as it is to social justice. Yet McGee *was* an honourable man, and he *was* an idealist, and there's no dirt against him at all except that he picked foolish quarrels and drank quite a bit (first for its own sake, then as anodyne to the crippling disease in his legs. When the whiskey interferred with his work, he quit. He supposedly died a teetotaller.).

I am neither a scholar nor an historian, yet it's impossible to separate McGee's life or ideas from his verse. His complete poems (assembled the year after his death by his friend Mary Sadlier) form his mind's autobiography, and a personal selection from that verse demands some kind of biographical overview.

For me it begins with Tommy McGee, the Irish *Rebell*. It is perhaps only in Ireland that radical, violent rebellion is nurtured by poetry, mythology and *Aislinn* – the vision of beauty – and succeeds through incompetent failure. McGee seems to have combined the natures of the four men singled out by Yeats in his

Easter 1916 memorial, the "Hearts with one purpose alone" who lost everything but created the "terrible beauty." He'd the history-steeped naivety and organisational flair of Padraig Pearse, the idealism and energy of Thomas Macdonagh, the rash aggressiveness of John MacBride, the egalitarian passion for justice of James Connelly. Add to these a pookish sense of fun. He was, this great Canadian whose far-flung obsequies formed the young nation's first communal rite, the most Irish of men.

McGee's rebellion was *The '48*. In that year of European revolutions it failed as ludicrously as any Irish insurgency – Cuchullain here stalked not through a post office but through Widow McCormack's cabbage patch – but like the later Easter Rising it lifted Ireland (devasted then by the potato famines and the bankruptcy of absentee landlords) one step closer to consciousness and freedom. And like the Easter Rising it had its roots in a literary movement.

This was Young Ireland, founded by the half-Welsh protestant, Thomas Davis, whose mouthpiece was *The Nation* (motto – "*Educate, that ye may be free*"). They were an astonishing group of men. Davis himself was a benign, rational genius, remembered if for nothing else in workaday Ireland now for what should be the national anthem: "A Nation Once Again." Charles Gavan Duffy, his successor, was acquitted of treason, moved to Australia and became within two years Prime Minister of the independent state of Victoria. Thomas Meagher ("Meagher of the Sword") had his death sentence commuted and was transported to Queensland. He escaped, found his way to New York, became a Union general in the Civil War, and then Governor of Montana (he too was probably murdered – pitched overboard into the Missouri one night in the year of Confederation). There was James Clarence Mangan, a junkie and morbid dreamer, whose Dark Rosaleen begat Yeats' Cathleen ni Houlihan. And there was Tommy McGee, smuggled out of Ireland with a bishop's connivance, disguised as a priest. D'Arcy McGee, editor, lecturer and historian. The Honourable Thomas D'Arcy McGee,

Father of Confederation, shot down as a traitor by his own tribe, whose collected poems fill more than 500 pages.

McGee never forgot Young Ireland, though he denounced their politics later as "youthful folly," and he never forgot the motto of *The Nation*. While he was running his own *New York Nation* in 1848-9 he worked tirelessly at creating, and then teaching in the "Night Schools" for working men. This passion for education and social justice earned him the name in Canada of "Friend of the Poor" (his last, voluntary act for Canada's parliament was to raise funds for the Nova Scotia fishermen whose '67 harvest had been disastrous) and led him to write "*The Mental Outfit of the New Dominion*," first delivered as a lecture in Montreal in November 1867. The message of that speech has the same bleak resonance today as his words to the House that April night the next year. It defined Canada's future in terms of mental vitality. It urged the encouragement of a literature "calculated to our own meridian, and hitting home our own society, either where it is sluggish or priggish, or wholly defective in its present style of culture," and hoped:

> if a native book should lack the finish of a foreign one,
> as a novice may well be less expert than an old hand, yet if
> the book be honestly designed, and conscientiously worked
> up, the author shall be encouraged, not only for his own
> sake, but for the sake of the better things which we look
> forward to with hopefulness. I make this plea on behalf of
> those who venture upon authorship among us because I
> believe the existence of a recognised literary class will by
> and by be felt as a state and social necesssity.

His best verse expresses the same ideals and indignations as that speech. "Peace Hath Her Victories" (a poem which carries its own ironies now that we "peacekeepers" have joined in the bombing in the Gulf) makes this equation:

> To raise the drooping artist's head, to breathe
>   The word despairing genius thirsts to hear,
> To crown all service with its earnest wreath,
>   To be of lawless force the foe austere;
> This is to stretch a sceptre over Time,
>   This is to give our darkling earth a star,
> And belt it with the emerald scroll sublime;
>   Peace hath her victories, no less than war.

Canada meant to McGee all the possibilities that the U.S. had betrayed: equality and opportunity for all citizens. He was appalled, after his first infatuation with Old Glory, at the nature of slavery (he ran a newspaper in Buffalo, the finland station of the underground railroad), at the corruption of politicians (above all the crude and cruel manipulation of their own people by Irish ward-bosses), at the bigotry and sectarianism, at rampant, exploitative capitalism, and at the bulldozing creed of "manifest destiny" (it was not just the Fenians who prepared to invade in the 1860's, and one of McGee's urgencies in campaigning for Confederation had been to keep American hands off the West).

It was contradictory to some, of course, (to the Fenians above all) this switch from rebellion to a belief in "Cause, Constitution, Country, King" but in his own words: "The British Flag does fly in Canada, but it throws no shadow," and again: "We are loyal because our equal civil, social and religious rights are respected. Were it otherwise, we would be otherwise." He was, after all, a traditionalist. He believed in Crown, Church and State, as he believed in the Social Contract.

It was this innate conservatism ("My native disposition is towards reverence for things old, and veneration for landmarks of the past") which led McGee to devote some of his prodigious energy to the writing of history. His "Popular History of Ireland" is still highly readable, and reliable. It was the hours spent in the British Museum reading room (when he should have been covering English parliamentary debates for the Dublin

Freeman) which persuaded him that the historian's role was as vital to a nation's consciousness as the poet's was. He devoured the newly published works of the antiquarians Eugene O'Curry and John O'Donovan, as well as translations from the Four Masters and of Keating (the best of which, irony of ironies, was by the Fenian leader John O'Mahoney). One result of this enthusiasm was that almost half of his poems are reworkings of Irish history.

Personally, I regret this. For me his sense of himself as an annalist was as much a deflection from his poetry as politics was. I have included no Irish historical poems in this selection.

McGee's best poetry, almost without exception, was a response to the immediate events of his time (underpinned, certainly, by an historical context), delivered with directness, wit and pungency and fuelled, more often than not, by indignation.

If the historical poems seem like conscientiously fulfilled duties, his best work is alive with energy and (even when the tone is outrage) with what can only be called high spirits. One of the delights in discovering McGee's verse is sharing the pleasure he took in writing it. He loves the language, he loves rhythm and rhyme and even at his most serious is aware that word-music of this sort has a gladness, even a merriment behind it. It can even, in its brisk dance-measures, achieve what can only be called "corniness" (in the sense that Mozart's horn concerti are corny). At such times, as in *When Fighting Was The Fashion*, the poem will take on its own tomfoolery life. The challenge of the feminine rhyme leads him to *flash on* and *dash on*, and *clash on* and *lash on* – yet the lament for past glories, and the final call to arms lose nothing for being rendered in this comical, quickstep mode. Always, inside McGee, there was a blithe satirist itching to get out.

It was his satirist's instinct, too, which gives his serious work its concrete, enduring qualities: the instinct to focus tone, diction and rhythm upon images rather than on ideas; images which carry both an immediate and an emblematic charge. The early poem, *Midsummer 1851*, for instance – despite its length, its historical scope and its threefold political argument – keeps all of its force today because the actualities of that long-past world are so vividly represented: visually precise, yet charged with the mocking fury of the poem:

> Why rusteth the swift bright sickle that swept down Saxon grain,
> Stuck in a patch of ragged thatch that keepeth not out the rain?

and Why lieth the plough on the headland with broken stilt and tusk?

and But go to the gate of Windsor, and ask its lady gay
> Why her Irish farm has gone to waste, and its farmers gone to clay.

and The robber knights are all around; from every castle-top
> They stretch their necks, a-hungering after the poor man's crop.

In the simplicity of the language, and the venomous, controlled rhythm, these images stand out and insist that we experience that world. They work, despite their simplicity, at several simultaneous levels; that will always be the hallmark of real poetry.

The received wisdom (insofar as anyone discusses McGee's verse these days) is that "To the last day of his life he wrote poems about Ireland. He tried to write about Canada but with only moderate success. The roots of his poetry were not in Canadian soil. The allegiance of the patriot could be willed, but not the poet's inspiration." (The words are Josephine Phelan's.) That is what I expected when I undertook this selection, but it turned out otherwise.

It seems to me that he wasted both time and talent on his Irish historical poems – time which he could ill afford, as a poet, given the pressures of public life, first as a journalist, then as a politician. All the same, the politics and the narrative versifying did, ironically, play their part in his development as a poet. For he *was* developing – he was a maturer writer at 40 than he had been at 30, and his experience of Canada was essential to that maturity.

My reasons for saying this are fourfold. Firstly, Canada gave his imagination new and concrete stimuli which produced lines more original than in even his most vivid Irish poems: confronted with new experiences, he recreates them without rhetoric. His response to the North, to cold, to ice and to snow was direct, not conventional. They were astonishments to him. His descriptions of icebergs, for instance, are precise and evocative:

> Lonely in nights of summer,
>   Beneath the starlight wan,
> A way-worn berg is met with,
>   Sad-featured as a man;
> All softly to the southward
>   Trailing its robes of white,
> It glides away with the current
>   Like a hooded Carmelite.

Similarly, his *The Death of Hudson* is infinitely better, to my taste, than any of his Irish or Classical narrative poems – because his imagination is really seized by the locale and by the challenge of telling a story *for the first time.*

Another night; uncheerily, beneath that heartless sky,
The iceberg sheds its livid light upon them passing by,
And each beholds the other's face, all spectre-like and wan,
And even in that dread solitude man fear'd the eye of man!
Afar they hear the beating surge sound from the banks of frost,
Many a hoar cape round about looms like a giant ghost,
And, fast or slow, as they float on, they hear the bears on shore
Trooping down to the icy strand, watching them evermore.

That, however melodramatic, is the real Arctic: concrete, tangible, an integral part of the narrative. And the narrative itself is charged with imaginative empathy and by the impulse to create a new, relevant mythology, rather that to preserve outworn ones.

Secondly, McGee's whole directness of speech was improved, I think, by the years of lecturing and debating, by the marrying of his amazing gift for impromptu eloquence to a direct approach and a persuasive strategy. He perceived poetry as public utterance and his best verse has the same qualities as his best speeches: it is clean and direct, its force does not come from bombast or loose melifluity, it neither pads nor prunes in subservience to form. A totally successful social poem, the sonnet *A Plea For The Poor*, is an example:

> 'Tis most true, madam! the poor wretch you turn'd
>   Forth from your door was not of aspect fair;
> His back was crooked, his eye, boa-like, burn'd,
>   Wild and inhuman hung his matted hair;
> His wit's unmannerly, uncouth his speech,
>   Awkward his gait; but, madam, pray recall
> How little Fate hath placed within his reach.
>   His lot in life – that may account for all.
> His bed hath been the inhospitable stones,
>   His canopy the weeping mists of night;
> Such savage shifts have warp'd his mind and bones,
>   And sent him all unseemly to your sight.
> Want is no courtier – Woe neglects all grace;
> He hunger'd, and he had it in his face!

That is a poem of indignation, of course, and from first to last (as I suggested earlier) McGee's best work was driven and shaped not by celebration but by outrage. This involves my third argument: by the time he was 40, McGee's political, religious and philosophical convictions were based upon experience, not just of life, but of *power*. He knew his aims and his targets now, precisely, and used none of the scatter-gun enthusiasm or simplifications of his youth.

But to return to *A Plea For The Poor* for a moment: it is an extremely accomplished poem technically, and not simply in its mastery of the sonnet form. The way that McGee's argument pivots and goes on the attack in the middle of a line (on the caesura of line six, in fact – exactly half way through the second quatrain of this Shakesperian sonnet –) is brilliant: this is the "turn" used with the technical assurance of a poet and an advocate. It is a piece which begs (like all his successful poems) to be read out aloud: and when read aloud, the tone and the voice take over, with all the modulations of feeling and thought which might be missed on the page.

There are wonderful games being played with language here, too: the vertical play of internal rhyme and half-rhyme, of consonance and assonance: *inhuman...matted...unmannerly... madam; gait...Fate; mists...shifts;* even, with an audacity which has no right to work (but here is that light-heartedness at work again), a series of *S* alliterations in the crucial last lines of the third quatrain – *Such savage shifts...sent...unseemly...sight* – which creates a spring-board for the last, taut couplet (with its concluding *H*-governed seven monosyllables!) that is loaded with hidden tension.

This is by way of introducing my fourth argument for McGee's development as a poet in his last years: he was not only improving but challenging his technical skills. He may not have been open to the real possibilities for modern poetry (as signposted, for example, by Whitman south of the border and Augusta Gregory back in Ireland: each in their different ways exploring the richness of colloquial language and folklore), but he was far from content with the forms he inherited. He was always a writer of verse (the distinction between verse and poetry is a recent one, and our age may be judged contemptuously as much for forgetting how to write verse as for its solipsistic, anecdotal, prosily doctrinaire "poetry") and he became increasingly skillful.

All the same, verse-forms – except for comic writers and

song-makers – become strait-jackets in the end. The struggle *between* content and form, the tension of working *against* restriction is what (since Hopkins) has most often made poetry out of verse. In his own way McGee was beginning to fight the restrictions of his own facile metre and rhymes. He experimented with Longfellow's unrhymed *Kalevala* rhythm and with some strangely subdued dactyllics *(Jacques Cartier And The Child)* and at last, in *Life A Mystery To Man*, found a craggy, flexible irregular blank verse which enabled the philosopher in him to say exactly what he meant. It is one of the great meditations of our culture. He remains a Victorian man, but his thought and verse are in mutiny against the available modes.

In making this selection I have chosen only poems which seem to me wholly successful in themselves (one of my frustrations has been the fitful brilliance – stanzas, lines, phrases, images – which enlivens even McGee's least memorable poems). So my choice is entirely an aesthetic one, uninfluenced by history, biography or politics.

The book is arranged more or less chronologically, and may give some sense of the intellectual and poetic development I've discussed, but there's no thematic shape here. And so some poems appear almost jarringly, because there are not enough of their kind to form a "movement" or suite. An example is *Grandma Alice*, a facetious romp reminiscent of Lewis Carrol which shows another side of McGee's personality, as well as his gift for extempore verse. *Christmas Morn* and *The Midnight Mass*, which precede *Life A Mystery To Man*, are examples of his childlike but far from primitive Catholicism ("The first great end of life is to be saved; And next, to leave the world the better for us."). There are also one or two pieces of willful Celtic morbidity (one wonders what Mary McGee made of poems on the graves of her perfectly healthy daughters, or of her own premature consignment to Heaven). There's no way to fit these poems into any sort of "scheme" – except the scheme of McGee's personality. The quirks are part of his charm. He contained his own small multitudes.

I'm not, honestly, sure about the two Jacques Cartier poems: in picking the first I may have been influenced by the subject matter and the fact that it's one of the two standard anthology pieces. *Jacques Cartier And The Child* is included, in part, to demonstrate the technical restlessness I mentioned above. Everything else, I believe, is here on its own merits.

Inevitably, I've become fond of D'Arcy McGee: discovering and choosing his poems, reading his speeches and the three excellent biographies has been an experience, in W.H. Auden's words, of "breaking bread with the dead." We were lucky to have him; we could certainly use him today. However much he might quarrel with my choice of his verse he would see it, I hope, as a gesture from our time towards his neglected life's work; a statement of his continued relevance; a realisation of the dream he described in *A Fragment*, for he should have the last word:

>   I dream'd a dream when the woods were green,
>   And my April heart made an April scene,
>   In the far, far distant land,
>   That even I might something do
>   That should keep my memory for the true
>   And my name from the spoiler's hand.

Selected Verse
of
THOMAS D'ARCY McGEE

IMPROMPTU

A happy bird that hung on high
In the parlor of the hostelry,
Where daily resorted ladies fair
To breathe the garden-perfumed air,
    And hear the sweet musician;
Removed to the public room at last,
His spirit seem'd quite overcast,
He lost his powers of tune and time,
As I did mine of rhythm and rhyme
    When I turn'd politican.

MIDSUMMER, 1851

Why standeth the laborer in the way, with sunken eyes and dim?
Is there no work, is there no hope, is there no help for him?
Why rusteth the swift, bright sickle that swept down Saxon grain,
Stuck in a patch of ragged thatch that keepeth not out the rain?

Why lieth the plough on the headland, with broken stilt and tusk?
Why gapeth the sun-dried furrow from gray dawn unto dusk?
Why cometh no singing sower, scattering song and seed,
Where the field-mouse rangeth fat and free amid his groves of weed?

There was no eathquake in the land—the ocean swept not here—
Since we beheld the grateful soil enrich the waning year;
The kind clouds in the west are throng, and hither bring their rain—
Now, why is the laborer lost for work, and the land disrobed of grain?

Ask not the peasant nor the priest—ask not the papers why—
Why would you shame the manly cheek, or fill the feeling eye—
But go to the gate of Windsor, and ask its lady gay
Why her Irish farm has gone to waste, and its farmers gone to clay.

Ah! if the sceptre had a soul, if conscience topp'd the crown,
We soon would have the truth made plain in country and in town—
Plain as the ancient mountains—plain as the girdling sea—
That in the laws lie all the cause of Ireland's misery.

You, Irish farmers, whose thin ranks are broken and dismay'd,
You know what spoil is made of toil, how all this woe is made;
The Lady of Windsor little thinks how you have rack'd and wrought
Your bones and brains to foster all that thus has gone to nought.

Little she knows that round her stand a gang of thievish earls,
Whose founts are fed, whose wines are cool'd with tears of humble churls;
Little she knows that to their gods of Rank and Fashion rise
Daily a litany of groans, and a human sacrifice!

The plough will rot, the furrow gape, the worker wait in vain,
Till Law and Labor, side by side, shall grapple Pride again.
Oh, Lady of Windsor, think betimes that even the strongest throne
May not withstand the just demand of Labor for "his own."

We ask no shares of Indian wealth, no spoils of Eastern shores;
Kaffir and Dyak still, for us, may heap and hide their stores;
We ask not London's pride and pomp, nor Yorkshire's iron arms—
We ask the law to guard and judge the farmers on their farms.

The robber knights are all around; from every castle-top
They stretch their necks, a-hungering after the poor man's crop:
We ask that Justice have her seat amid the upstack'd corn,
That all he sowed and nursed may not from Labor's grasp be torn.

Is this too much? Is this a crime? Let men and angels judge.
Hark to the lords' hired advocate, but hear us for the drudge;
Between our causes let the state in lawfulness preside,
And we will gladly take the share awarded to our side.

Hear us and judge, while yet on earth our fiery race remain;
"Too late" can never be unsaid, nor even said in vain.
To the far West—to God's own court—already hosts are fled;—
Oh hear and save the living left, ere again "too late" be said!

A MALEDICTON

"My native land! how does it fare
   Since last I saw its shore?"
"Alas! alas! my exiled frère,
   It aileth more and more.
God curse the knaves who yearly steal
   The produce of its plains;
Who for the poor man never feel,
   Yet gorge on labor's gains!

"We both can well recall the time
   When Ireland yet was gay;
It needed then no wayside sign
   To show us where to stay.
A stranger sat by ev'ry hearth,
   At ev'ry board he fed;
It was a work of maiden mirth
   To make the wanderer's bed.

"'Tis altered times: at every turn
   A shiftless gang you meet;
The hutless peasants starve and mourn,
   Camp'd starkly in the street.
The warm old homes that we have known
   Went down like ships at sea;
The gateless pier, the cold hearth-stone,
   Their sole memorials be.

"We two are old in years and woes,
   And Age has powers to dread;
And now, before our eyes we close,
   Our malison be said:
The curse of two gray-headed men
   Be on the cruel crew*
Who've made our land a wild-beast's den—
   And God's curse on them too."

*Meaning the "exterminating" landlords. [*T.D.M.*]

SONG OF THE SURPLUS

The oak-trees wave around the hall,
   The dock and thistle own the lea,
The hunter has his air-tight stall,
   But there's no place for such as me;
The rabbit burrows in the hill,
   The fox is scarce begrudged his den,
The cattle crop the pasture still,
   But our masters have "no room for men."

Each thing that lives may live in peace—
   The browsing beast and bird of air;
No torturers are train'd for these,
   While man's life is a long despair.
The Lady Laura's eyes are wet
   If her dog dies beneath her feet;
It has its burial rites—and yet
   Our human griefs no mercy meet.

Well may'st thou ask, O Preacher true,
   Of manly sense and fearless tongue—
Like Israel's prophet, well may you
   Exclaim, "How long, Oh Lord! how long?"
How long may Fraud and Pride, and Power
   Conspire to slay the immortal soul?
How long shall Ireland groan and cower
   Beneath this thrice-accursed control?

When shall we see free homes abound,
   And meet by street, and bridge, and stile,
The freeman's lifted brow unbow'd,
   As free from guilt, as free from guile?
The song of peace, the hum of toil
   Will flow along our rivers when?
When none within our native isle
   Shall say, we have "no room for men."

THE EXILE'S MEDITATION

Alone in this mighty city, queen of the continent!
I ponder on my people's fate in grief and discontent—
Alas! that I have lived to see them wiled and cast away,
And driven like soulless cattle from their native land a prey.

These men, are they not our brethren, grown at our mother's breast?
Are they not come of the Celtic blood, in Europe held the best?
And they not heirs of Brian, and children of Eoghan's race,
Who rose up like baited tigers and sprung in the foeman's face?

And why should they seek another shore, to live in another land?
Had they not plenty at their feet, and sickles in their hand?
Did an eathquake march upon them, did Nature make them flee,
Or do they fly for fear, and to seek some ready-made Liberty?

I have read in ancient annals of a race of gallant men
Who fear'd neither Dane nor devil; but it is long since then—
And "cowardice is virtue," so runs the modern creed—
The starving suicide is praised and sainted for the deed!

DEEDS DONE IN DAYS OF SHAME

A deed! a deed! O God, vouchsafe,
   Which shall not die with me,
But which may bear my memory safe
   O'er time's wreck-spotted sea,—
A deed, upon whose brow shall stand
   Traced, large in lines of flame—
"This hath been done for Ireland,
   Done in the days of shame!"

An age will come, when Fortune's sun
   Will beam in Ireland's sky,
And mobs of flatterers then will run
   To hail her majesty.
Amid that crowd I shall not be
   To join in the acclaim;
But deeds will have their memory,
   Though done in days of shame.

When six feet of a stranger soil
   Shall press upon my heart,
And envy's self will pause awhile
   To praise the manly part—
Oh ye who rise in Ireland, then,
   To fight your way to fame,
Think of the deeds by mouldering men
   Done in the days of shame!

"WHEN FIGHTING WAS THE FASHION"

We've ships of steam, and we have wires
    Thought travels like a flash on—
But much we've lost that was our sires',
    When fighting was the fashion.

Oh gay and gentle was their blood—
    Who Danes and Dutch did dash on,
Who to the last all odds withstood,
    When fighting was the fashion.

The grain that grew in Ireland then,
    Their own floors they did thrash on—
They lived and died like Christian men,
    When fighting was the fashion.

Then Milan mail, in many a field,
    Mountmellick swords did clash on,
And generals to our chiefs did yield,
    When fighting was the fashion.

But now, oh shame! we lick the hand
    That daily lays the lash on—
Luck never can befall our land,
    Till fighting comes in fashion.

THE REAPER'S SONG

Air—*The Jolly Shearers*

The August sun is setting
   Like a fire behind the hills—
'Twill rise again to see us free
   Of life or of its ills;
For what is life, but deadly strife
   That knows no truce or pause,
And what is death, but want of breath
   To curse their alien laws?
      Chorus—Then a-shearing let us go, my boys,
         A-shearing let us go,
         On our own soil 'twill be no toil
         To lay the corn low.

The harvest that is growing
   Was given us by God—
Praise be to Him, the sun and shower
   Work'd for us at his nod.
The lords of earth, in gold and mirth,
   Ride on their ancient way,
But could their smile have clothed the isle
   In such delight to-day?
     Chorus.

"How will you go a-shearing,
   Dear friends and neighbors all?"
"Oh, we will go with pike and gun,
   To have our own or fall;
We'll stack our arms and stack our corn
   Upon the same wide plain;
We'll plant a guard in barn and yard,
   And give them grape for grain."
     Chorus.

God speed ye, gallant shearers,
  May your courage never fail,
May you thrash your foes, and send the chaff
  To England on the gale!
May you have a glorious harvest-home,
  Whether I'm alive or no;
Your corn grows *here*, the foe comes *there*—
  Or *it* or *he* must go.
    Chorus—Then a-shearing let us go, my boys,
      A-shearing we will go,
      On our own soil 'twill be no toil
      To cut the corn low.

THE EXILE'S DEVOTION

If I forswear the art divine
    Which deifies the dead—
What comfort then can I call mine,
    What solace seek instead?
For, from my birth, our country's fame
    Was life to me and love,
And for each loyal Irish name
    Some garland still I wove.

I'd rather be the bird that sings
    Above the martyr's grave,
Than fold in fortune's cage my wings
    And feel my soul a slave;
I'd rather turn one simple verse
    True to to the Gaelic ear,
Than classic odes I might rehearse
    With senates list'ning near.

Oh, native land! dost ever mark
    When the world's din is drown'd,
Betwixt the daylight and the dark
    A wondering, solemn sound
That on the western wind is borne
    Across thy dewy breast?
It is the voice of those who mourn
    For thee, far in the West.

For them and theirs I oft essay
    Your ancient art of song,
And often sadly turn away
    Deeming my rashness wrong;
For well I ween, a loving will
    Is all the art I own;
Ah me! could love suffice for skill,
    What triumphs I had known!

My native land! my native land!
    Live in my memory still;
Break on my brain, ye surges grand!
    Stand up! mist-cover'd hill.
Still in the mirror of the mind
    The scenes I love I see;
Would I could fly on the western wind,
    My native land! to thee.

THE HEART'S RESTING-PLACE

Twice have I sail'd the Atlantic o'er,
    Twice dwelt an exile in the West;
Twice did kind nature's skill restore
    The quiet of my troubled breast—
As moss upon a rifted tree,
    So time its gentle cloaking did,
But though the wound no eye could see,
    Deep in my heart the barb was hid.

I felt a weight where'er I went—
    I felt a void within my brain;
My day-hopes and my dreams were blent
    With sable threads of mental pain;
My eye delighted not to look
    On forest old or rapids grand;
The stranger's joy I scare could brook—
    My heart was in my own dear land.

Where'er I turn'd, some emblem still
    Roused consciousness upon my track;
Some hill was like an Irish hill,
    Some wild bird's whistle call'd me back;
A sea-bound ship bore off my peace
    Between its white, cold wings of woe;
Oh! if I had but wings like these,
    Where my peace went I too would go.

EXECUTION OF ARCHBISHOP PLUNKETT

London, July, 1681

Another scaffold looms up through the night,
    Another Irish martyr's hour draws near,
The cruel crowd are gathering for the sight,
    The July day dawns innocently clear;
There is no hue of blood along the sky,
Where the meek martyr waits for light to die!

Which is the culprit in the car of death?
    He of the open brow and folded hands!
The turbid crowd court every easy breath,
    There is no need on him of gyves or bands;
Pale, with long bonds and vigils, yet benign,
He bears upon his breast salvation's sign.

What was his crime? Did he essay to shake
    The pillar of the state, or undermine
The laws which vow a worthy vengeance,
    And punish treason with a death condign?
Look in that holy face, and there behold
The secret of the sufferer's life all told.

Enough! he was of Irish birth and blood,
    He fill'd Saint Patrick's place in stormy days,
He lived, discharging duty, doing good,
    Dead to the world, and the world's idle praise, —
The faithless saw his faith with evil eyes,
They doom'd him without stain, and here he dies.

THE THREE MINSTRELS

Three Minstrels play within the Tower of Time,
    A weird and wondrous edifice it is:
One sings of war, the martial strain sublime,
    And strikes his lyre as 'twere a foe of his.
The sword upon his thigh is dripping red
    From a foe's heart in the mid-battle slain;
His plumèd casque is doff'd from his proud head,
    His flashing eye preludes the thundrous strain.

Apart, sequester'd in an alcove deep,
    Through which the pale moon looks propitious in,
Accompanied by sighs that seem to weep,
    The second minstrel sadly doth begin
To indite his mistress fair, but cruel, who
    Had trampled on the heart that was her own;
Or prays his harp to help him how to woo,
    And thrills with joy at each responsive tone.

Right in the porch, before which, fair and far,
    Plain, lake, and hamlet fill the musing eye,
Gazing toward the thoughtful evening star
    That seems transfixed upon the mountain high,
The third of Country and of Duty sings:
    Slow and triumphal is the solemn strain;
Like Death, he takes no heed of chiefs or kings,
    But over all he maketh Country reign.

Sad Dante. he, love-led from life, who found
    His way to Eden, and unhappy stood
Amid the angels—he, the cypress-crown'd,
    Knew not the utmost gift of public good.
Thoughts deeper and more solemn it inspires
    Than even his lofty spirit dare essay;
How then shall we, poor Emberers of old fires,
    Kindle the beacons of our country's way?

We all are audience in the Tower of Time;
    For us alone at this hour play the three,—
Choose which ye will—the martial song sublime,
    Or lover fond; but thou my Master be,
O Bard of Duty and of Country's cause!
    Thee will I choose and follow for my lord!
Thy theme my study and thy words my laws—
    Muse of the patriot lyre and guardian sword!

LORD GL—GALL'S DREAM

A dream which was not all a dream. – *Byron*.

Lord Gl—Gall slept in "the House" last night,
When a terrible vision oppress'd his sight;
'Twas not of Incumber'd Estates ('tis said),
Nor the Durham Bull, nor the hat so red—
But he dreamt that a balance he saw in air,
Above the broad Curragh of famed Kildare—
That God and the landlords both were there.

He heard the recording angel call
The titled criminals one and all,
And the witnesses to testify—
And he heard the four far winds reply;
And myriads heap'd on myriads throng
From unnumber'd graves to denounce the wrong,
And with their sins to confront the strong!

His lordship scarce could tell for fear,
Of every name that met his ear;
But he saw that the archangel took
Note of them all in his blackest book—
From Farney some, and from Skibbereen,
From West and East and the lands between,
Such a skeleton tryst has never been seen.

He heard how Sir George gave the widow's mite
As instalment to a sybarite—
He heard how Lord Dick his fox-hounds fed
With ten starved cottiers' daily bread—
Anon, he trembled to hear his own
Name, named in the angel's sternest tone,
And thereat, upstarted he with a groan.

Sadly he paces his silent hall,
Still muttering over the name Gl—Gall—
And penitent thoughts depress his head,
But the grave will not give up its dead.
Far, far away from their native Suir
Are scatter'd the bones of the exiled poor,
But the angel has note of them all, be sure!

THE MAN OF THE NORTH COUNTRIE

He came from the North and his words were few,
But his voice was kind and his heart was true,
And I knew by his eyes no guile had he,
So I married the man of the North Countrie.

Oh! Garryowen may be more gay,
Than this quiet street of Ballibay;
And I know the sun shines softly down
On the river that passes my native town.

But there's not—I say it with joy and pride—
Better man than mine in Munster wide;
And Limerick Town has no happier hearth
Than mine has been with my Man of the North.

I wish that in Munster they only knew
The kind, kind neighbors I came unto;
Small hate or scorn would ever be
Between the South and the North Countrie.

THE CELT'S PRAYER

Oh, King of Heaven! who dwelleth throned afar
Beyond the hills, the skylark, and the star,
Whose ear was never shut to our complaints,
Look down and hear the children of thy Saints!

We ask no strength of arm, or heart, O Lord!
We still can hoist the sail and ply the sword,
We ask no gifts of grain—our soil still bears
Abundant harvests to the fruitful years!

The gift, O Lord, we need, to David's son
You gave, for asking, once in Gabaon;
The gift of Wisdom, which, of all your powers,
Most needful is, dread Lord! to us and ours!

Our race was mighty once, when at their head
Wise men, like steadfast torches, burn'd and led;
When Ollamh's lore and royal Cormac's spell
Guided the Gael, all things with them went well.

Finn, famed for courage, was more famed for art,
For frequent meditations made apart;
Dathi and Nial, valorous both and sage,
Were slow in anger, seldom stirr'd to rage.

Look down on us, oh Sire, and hear our cries!
Grant to our chiefs the courage to be wise,
Endow them with a wisdom from Thy throne,
That they may yet restore to us our own!

THE TRIP OVER THE MOUNTAIN

A Popular Ballad of Wexford

'Twas night, and the moon was just seen in the west,
   When I first took a notion to marry;
I rose and pursued my journey in haste,
   You'd have known that I was in a hurry.
I came to the door, and I rattled the pin,
I lifted the latch and did boldly walk in,
And seeing my sweetheart, I bid her "good e'en,"
      Saying, "Come with me over the mountain!"

"What humor is this you've got in your head,
   I'm glad for to see you so merry;
It's twelve by the clock, and they're all gone to bed:
   Speak low, or my dadda will hear ye!"
"I've spoken my mind, and I never will rue;
I've courted a year, and I think it will do;
But if you refuse me, sweet girl, adieu!
      I must go alone over the mountain!"

"But if from my dadda and mamma I go,
   They never will think of me longer;
The neighbors about them, too, will not be slow
   To say, that no one could do wronger."
"Sweet girl, we're wasting the sweet hours away,
I care not a fig what the whole of them say,
For you will be mine by the dawn of the day,
      If you'll come with me over the mountain!"

She look'd in my face with a tear in her eye,
    And saw that my mind was still steady,
Then rubb'd out the tear she was going to cry;
    "In God's name, my dear, now get ready!"
"Stop! stop! a few moments, till I get my shoes!"
My heart it rejoiced for to hear the glad news;
She lifted the latch, saying, "I hope you'll excuse
    My simplicity, over the mountain!"

'Twas night, and the moon had gone down in the west,
    And the morning star clearly was shining,
As we two pursued our journey in haste,
    And were join'd at the altar of Hymen!
In peace and contentment we spent the long day,
The anger of parents, it soon wore away,
And oft we sat chatting, when we'd nothing to say,
    Of the trip we took over the mountain!

THE PRAYER TO ST. BRENDAN

Upon this sea a thousand dolphins swam,
    Tossing their nostrils up to breathe awhile;
And here the lumbering leviathan,
    Lay heap'd and long like some half-founder'd isle;
When, from the west, a low and antique sail
    Swell'd with soft winds that wafted prayers before,
Bore thy frail bark, Columbus of the Gael,
    Far from thy native Connaught's sheltering shore!

Mo-Brendan! Saint of Sailors! list to me,
    And give thy benediction to our bark,
For still, they say, thou savest souls at sea,
    And lightest signal-fires in tempest dark.
Thou sought'st the Promised Land far in the West,
    Earthing the sun, chasing Hesperion on,
But we in our own Ireland had been blest,
    Nor ever sigh'd for land beyond the sun!

Shores of eternal spring might cross in vain,
    For all the odious wealth we counted nought;
The birds-of-paradise might sing in vain,
    Had not our cup with too much woe been fraught!
Then, sailing in thy legendary wake,
    We lift our hearts and voices unto thee;
Bless the far realm that for our spirits' sake
    You sought of yore through the untravell'd sea!

And for us, outcasts for the self-same cause,
    Beseech from Heaven's full granary some store
Of grace to love and fear the equal laws
    Enthroned upon that liberated shore.
Help us to dwell in brotherhood and love,
    In the New Home predestined for our race;
So may our souls to thine, in heaven above,
    Pass glorified, through their great Master's grace!

AN INVITATION WESTWARD

Ye are weary, O my people, of your warfare and your woes,
In the island of your birthright every seed of sorrow grows;
Hearken to me, come unto me, where your wearied souls may rest
And plume their wings in peace, in the forests of the West.

This life—ah! what avails it by which shore we may be led
To the mounds where lie entrench'd all the army of the dead?
In the Valley of All Souls, when the Lord of judgment comes,
The Cross shall be our banner, our country all the tombs.

Is it wise to waste the present in a future of the brain?
Is it wise to cling and wither under Mammon's deadly reign?
If the spirit of the toiler is by daily hate oppress'd,
How shall he pray to Heaven, as we do in the West?

It grieves my soul to say it—to say to you, Arise!
To follow where the evening star sings vespers down the skies;
It grieves my soul to call you from the land you love the best—
But I love Freedom better, and her home is now the West.

Then, children of Milesius, from your house of death arise,
And follow where the evening star sings vespers to the skies;
Though it grieve your souls to part from the land you love the best,
Fair Freedom will console you in the forests of the West.

On Lake Erie, September, 1852. [*T.D.M.*]

IT IS EASY TO DIE

       It is easy to die
           When one's work is done—
      To pass from the earth
          Like a harvest day's sun,
After opening the flowers and ripening the grain
Round the homes and the scenes where our friends remain.

       It is easy to die
           When one's work is done—
      Like Simeon, the priest,
          Who saw God's Son;
In the fulness of years, and the fulness of faith,
It is easy to sleep on the clay couch of death.

      But 'tis hard to die
          While one's native land
      Has scarce strength to cry
          'Neath the spoiler's hand;
O merciful God! vouchsafe that I
May see Ireland free,—then let me die.

TO MY WISHING-CAP

Wishing-cap, Wishing-cap, I would be
Far away, far away o'er the sea,
Where the red birch roots
Down the ribbed rock shoots,
   In Donegal the brave,
     And white-sail'd skiffs
      Speckle the cliffs,
   And the gannet drinks the wave.

Wishing-cap, Wishing-cap, I would lie
On a Wicklow hill, and stare the sky,
Or count the human atoms that pass
The thread-like road through Glenmacnass,
   Where once the clans of O'Bryne were;
     Or talk to the breeze
      Under sycamore trees,
   In Glenart's forests fair.

Wishing-cap, Wishing-cap, let us away
To walk in the cloisters, at close of day,
Once trod by friars of orders gray,
In Norman Selskar's renown'd abbaye,
   And Carmen's ancient town;
For I would kneel at my mother's grave,
Where the plumy churchyard elms wave,
   And the old war-walls look down.

SONNET—RETURN

I have a sea-going spirit haunts my sleep,
    Not a sad spirit wearisome to follow,
Less like a tenant of the mystic deep
    Than the good fairy of the hazel hollow;
Full often at the midwatch of the night
    I see departing in his silver bark
This spirit, steering toward an Eastern light,
    Calling me to him from the Western dark.
"Spirit!" I ask, "say, whither bound away?"
    "Unto the old Hesperides!" he cries.
"Oh, Spirit, take me in thy bark, I pray."
    "For thee I came," he joyfully replies;
"Exile! no longer shalt thou absent mourn,
For I the Spirit am men call—RETURN."

THE IRISH HOMES OF ILLINOIS

Chorus—The Irish homes of Illinois,
The happy homes of Illinois;
No landlord there
Can cause despair,
Nor blight our fields in Illinois.

'Tis ten good years since Ellen *bawn*
  Adventured with her Irish boy
Across the sea, and settled on
  A prairie farm in Illinois.
      The Irish homes of Illinois, etc.

Sweet waves the sea of summer flowers
  Around our wayside cot so coy,
Where Ellen sings away the hours
  That light my task in Illinois.
      The Irish homes of Illinois, etc.

Another Ellen's at her knee,
  And in her arms a laughing boy;
And I bless God to see them free
  From want and care in Illinois.
      The Irish homes of Illinois, etc.

And yet some shadows often steal
  Upon our hours of purest joy;
When happiest we most must feel
"If Ireland were like Illinois!"
      The Irish homes of Illinois, etc.

THE SHANTY

This is our castle! enter in,
    Sit down and be at home, sir;
Your city friend will do, I hope,
    As travellers do in Rome, sir!
'Tis plain the roof is somewhat low,
    The sleeping-room but scanty,
Yet to the Settler's eye, you know,
    His castle is—his Shanty!

The Famine fear we saw of old,
    Is, like a nightmare, over;
That wolf will never break our fold,
    Nor round the doorway hover.
Our swine in droves tread down the brake,
    Our sheep-bells carol canty,
Last night yon salmon swam the lake,
    That now adorns our Shanty.

That bread we break, it is our own,
    It grew around my feet, sir,
It pays no tax to Squire or Crown,
    Which makes it doubly sweet, sir!
A woodman leads a toilsome life,
    And a lonely one, I grant ye,
Still, with his children, friend, and wife,
    How happy is his Shanty!

No feudal lord o'erawes us here,
    Save the Ever-bless'd Eternal;
To Him is due the fruitful year,
    Both autumnal and vernal;
We've rear'd to Him, down in the dell,
    A temple, neat, though scanty,
And we can hear its blessed bell
    On Sunday, in our Shanty.

This is our castle! enter in,
    Sit down, and be at home, sir;
Your city friend will do, I hope,
    As travellers do in Rome, sir!
'Tis plain the roof is somewhat low,
    The sleeping-room but scanty,
Yet to the Settler's eye, you know,
His castle is—his Shanty!

"THE ARMY OF THE WEST"

We fight upon a new-found plan, our Army of the West—
Our brave brigades, along the line, will leave the foe no rest—
Our battle-axes, bright and keen, with every day's swift sands,
Lay low the foes of Liberty, and then annex their lands;
On, onward through the Western woods our standard saileth ever
And shadows many a nameless peak and unbaptizèd river—
The Army of the Future we, the champions of the Unborn—
We pluck the primal forests up, and sow their sites with corn.

That rugged standard beareth the royal arms of toil—
The axe, and pike, and ponderous sledge, and plough that frees the soil—
The field is made of stripes, and the stars the crest supplies,
And the living eagles hover round the flag-staffs where it flies.
And thus beneath our standard, right merrily we go,
The Future for our heritage, the tangled Waste our foe;
The Army of the Future we, the champions of the Unborn—
We pluck the primal forests up, and sow their sites with corn.

Down in yon glade the anvil rings beneath the arching oaks,
Behind yon hills our neighbors drive the oxen in the yokes,
Yon laughing boys now boating down the rapid river's tide,
Go to the learnèd man who keeps the log-house on its side—
Like suckers of the pine they grow, elastic, rugged, tall,
They will hit a swallow on the wing with a single rifle ball—
The cadets of our army they, from "the West-Point" of the unborn,
They too will pluck the forests up, and sow their sites with corn.

Oh ye who dwell in cities, in the self-conceited East,
Do you ever think how by our toils your comforts are increased?
When you walk upon your carpets, and sit on your easy chairs,
And read self-applauding stories, and give yourselves such airs—
Do you ever think upon us, Backwoodsmen of the West,
Who, from the Lakes to Texas, have given the foe no rest?
On the Army of the Future, and the champions of the Unborn,
Who pluck the primal forests up, and sow their sites with corn?

A SALUTATION
TO THE FREE FLAG OF AMERICA

Flag of the Free! I remember me well
   When your stars in our dark sky were shining—
'Twas the season when men like cold rain fell,
   And pour'd into graves unrepining—
'Twas the season when darkness and death rode about
   In the eye of the day dim with sorrow,
And the mourner's son had scarce strength to moan out
   Ere he follow'd his sire on the morrow.

Flag of the Free! I beheld you again,
   And I bless'd God who guarded me over—
And I found in your shade that the children of men
   Half the glory of Adam recover.
And they tell me, the knaves! thou doest typify sin,
   That thy folds fling infection around them,
That thy stars are but spots of the plague that's within,
   And which shortly will raging surround them.

Not so! oh, not so! thou bright pioneer banner!
   Thou art not what factions miscall thee;
Where Humanity is there must ever be Honor—
   Shame cannot stain let what else may befall thee:
Over Washington's march, o'er the Macedon's freight
   When flying, the angels ordain'd thee—
"The Flag of the Free, the belovèd of Fate,
And the hope of Mankind," have they named thee!

FREEDOM'S JOURNEY

Freedom! a nursling of the North,
   Rock'd in the arms of stormy pines,
On fond adventure wander'd forth
   Where south the sun superbly shines;
      The prospect shone so bright and fair,
      She dreamt her home was there, was there.

She lodged 'neath many a gilded roof,
   They gave her praise in many a hall,
Their kindness check'd the free reproof,
   Her heart dictated to let fall;
      She heard the Negro's helpless prayer,
      And felt her home could not be there.

She sought through rich savannas green,
   And in the proud palmetto grove,
But where her altar should have been
   She found nor liberty nor love;
      A cloud came o'er her forehead fair,
      She found no shrine to Freedom there.

Back to her native scenes she turn'd,
   Back to the hardy, kindly North,
Where bright aloft the pole-star burn'd,
   Where stood her shrine by every hearth;
      "Back to the North I will repair,"
      The goddess cried; "my home is there!"

ALONG THE LINE

A.D. 1812

Steady be your beacon's blaze
    Along the line! along the line!
Freely sing dear Freedom's praise
    Along the line! along the line!
Let the only sword you draw
Bear the legend of the law,
Wield it less to strike than awe
    Along the line! along the line!

Let them rail against the North
    Beyond the line! beyond the line!
When it sends its heroes forth
    Along the line! along the line!
On the field or in the camp
They shall tremble at your tramp,
Men of the old Norman stamp,
    Along the line! along the line!

Wealth and pride may rear their crests,
    Beyond the line! beyond the line!
They bring no terror to our breasts,
    Along the line! along the line!
We have never bought or sold
Afric's sons with Mexic's gold,
Conscience arms the free and bold,
    Along the line! along the line!

Steadfast stand, and sleepless ward,
    Along the line! along the line!
Great the treasures that you guard
    Along the line! along the line!
By the babes whose sons shall be
Crown'd in far futurity
With the laurels of the free,
    Stand your guard along the line!

ICEBERGS

Steamer Albion, Lat. 46.55 N., Long. 52.30 W

Parting their arctic anchors
   The bergs came drifting by,
A fearful fleet for a ship to meet
   Under the midnight sky;
Their keels are fathoms under,
   Their prows are sharp as steel,
Their stroke, the crash of thunder,
   All silently on they steal.

In the ruddy glow of daylight,
   When the sea is clear and wide,
When the sun with a clear and gay light
   Gilds the avalanche's side;
Then the sailor-boy sees castles
   And cities fair to view,
With battlements and archways
   And horsemen riding through.

Lonely in nights of summer,
   Beneath the starlight wan,
A way-worn berg is met with,
   Sad-featured as a man;
All softly to the southward
   Trailing its robes of white,
It glides away with the current
   Like a hooded Carmelite.

To-day—'twas Sunday evening—
   When dimly from the north,
Under the far horizon
   A church-like cloud came forth;
It came, a white reminder
   Of the memories of the day;
As a silent sign, we fancied,
   It paused, and pass'd its way.

Sunday, 19th May, 1867.

THE DEATH OF HUDSON

The slayer *Death* is everywhere, and many a mask hath he,
Many and awful are the shapes in which he sways the sea;
Sometimes within a rocky aisle he lights his candle dim,
And sits half-sheeted in the foam, chanting a funeral hymn;
Full oft amid the roar of winds we hear his awful cry,
Guiding the lightning to its prey through the beclouded sky;
Sometimes he hides 'neath Tropic waves, and, as the ship sails o'er,
He holds her fast to the fiery sun, till the crew can breathe no more.

There is no land so far away but he meeteth mankind there—
He liveth at the icy pole with the 'berg and the shaggy bear,
He smileth from the southern capes like a May queen in her flowers,
He falleth o'er the Indian seas, dissolved in summer showers;
But of all the sea-shapes he hath worn, may mariners never know
Such fate as Heinrich Hudson found, in the labyrinths of snow—
The cold north seas' Columbus, whose bones lie far interr'd
Under those frigid waters where no song was ever heard.

'Twas when he sail'd from Amsterdam, in the adventurous quest
Of an ice-shored strait, through which to reach the far and fabled West;
His dastard crew—their thin blood chill'd beneath the Arctic sky—
Combined against him in the night; his hands and feet they tie,
And bind him in a helmless boat, on that dread sea to sail—
Ah, me! an oarless, shadowy skiff, as a schoolboy's vessel frail.
Seven sick men, and his only son, his comrades were to be,
But ere they left the Crescent's side, the chief spoke, dauntlessly:

"Ho, mutineers! I ask no act of kindness at your hands—
My fate I feel must steer me to Death's still-silent lands;
But there is one man in my ship who sail'd with me of yore,

By many a bay and headland of the New World's eastern shore;
From India's heats to Greenland's snows he dared to follow me,
And is HE turn'd traitor too, is HE in league with ye?"
Uprose a voice from the mutineers, "Not I, my chief, not I—
I'll take my old place by your side, though all be sure to die."

Before his chief could bid him back, he is standing at his side;
The cable's cut—away they drift, over the midnight tide.
No word from any lip came forth, their strain'd eyes steadily
    glare
At the vacant gloom, where late the ship had left them to despair.
On the dark waters long was seen a line of foamy light—
It pass'd, like the hem of an angel's robe, away from their eager
    sight.
Then each man grasp'd his fellow's hand, some sigh'd, but none
    could speak,
While on, through pallid gloom, their boat drifts moaningly and
    weak.

Seven sick men, dying, in a skiff five hundred leagues from shore!
Oh! never was such a crew afloat on this world's waves before;
Seven stricken forms, seven sinking hearts of seven short-
    breathing men,
Drifting over the sharks' abodes, along to the white bear's den.
Oh! 'twas not there they could be nursed in homeliness and ease!
One short day heard seven bodies sink, whose souls God rest in
    peace!
The one who first expired had most to note the foam he made,
And no one pray'd to be the last, though each the blow delay'd.

Three still remained. "My son! my son! hold up your head, my
    son!
Alas! alas! my faithful mate, I fear his life is gone."
So spoke the trembling father—two cold hands in his breast,
Breathing upon his dead boy's face, all too soft to break his rest.

The roar of battle could not wake that sleeper from his sleep;
The trusty sailor softly lets him down to the yawning deep;
The fated father hid his face while this was being done,
Still murmuring mournfully and low, "My son, my only son."

Another night; uncherrily, beneath that heartless sky,
The iceberg sheds its livid light upon them passing by,
As each beholds the other's face, all spectre-like and wan,
And even in that dread solitude man fear'd the eye of man!
Afar they hear the beating surge sound from the banks of frost,
Many a hoar cape round about looms like a giant ghost,
And, fast or slow, as they float on, they hear the bears on shore
Trooping down to the icy strand, watching them evermore.

The morning dawns; unto their eyes the light hath lost its cheer;
Nor distant sail, nor drifting spar within their ken appear.
Embay'd in ice the coffin-like boat sleeps on the waveless tide,
Where rays of deathly-cold, cold light converge from every side.
Slow crept the blood into their hearts, each manly pulse stood
 still,
Huge haggard bears kept watch above on every dazzling hill.
Anon the doom'd men were entranced, by the potent frigid air,
And they dream, as drowning men have dreamt, of fields far off
 and fair.

What phantoms fill'd each cheated brain, no mortal ever knew;
What ancient storms they weather'd o'er, what seas explored
 anew;
What vast designs for future days—what home hope, or what
 fear—
There was no one 'mid the ice-lands to chronicle or hear.
So still they sat, the weird-faced seals bethought them they were
 dead,
And each raised from the waters up his cautious wizard head,
Then circled round the arrested boat, like vampires round a
 grave,

Till frighted at their own resolve—they plunged beneath the wave.

Evening closed round the moveless boat, still sat entranced the twain,
When lo! the ice unlocks its arms, the tide pours in amain!
Away upon the streaming brine the feeble skiff is borne,
The shaggy monsters howl behind their farewells all forlorn.
The crashing ice, the current's roar, broke Hudson's fairy spell,
But never more shall this world wake his comrade tried so well!
His brave heart's blood is chill'd for aye, yet shall its truth be told,
When the memories of kings are worn from marble and from gold.

Onward, onward, the helpless chief—the dead man for his mate!
The shark far down in ocean's depth feels the passing of that freight,
And bounding from his dread abyss, he snuffs the upper air,
Then follows on the path it took, like lion from his lair.
O God! it was a fearful voyage and fearful company,
Nor wonder that the stout sea-chief quiver'd from brow to knee.
Oh! who would blame his manly heart, if e'en *it* quaked for fear,
While whirl'd along on such a sea, with such attendant near!

The shark hath found a readier prey, and turn'd him from the chase;
The boat hath *made* another bay—a drearier pausing place—
O'er arching piles of blue-vein'd ice admitted to its still,
White, fathomless waters, palsied like the doom'd man's fetter'd will.
Powerless he sat—that chief escaped so oft by sea and land—
Death breathing o'er him—all so weak he could not lift a hand.
Even his bloodless lips refused a last short prayer to speak,
But angels listen at the heart when the voice of man is weak.

His heart and eye were suppliant turn'd to the ocean's Lord on high,
The Borealis lustres were gathering in the sky;
From South and North, from East and West, they cluster'd o'er the spot
Where breathed his last the gallant chief whose grave man seeth not;
They mark'd him die with steadfast gaze, as though in hèaven there were
A passion to behold how he the fearful fate would bear;
They watch'd him through the livelong night—these couriers of the sky,
Then fled to tell the listening stars how 'twas they saw him die.

He sleepeth where old Winter's realm no genial air invades,
His spirit burneth bright in heaven among the glorious shades,
Whose God-like doom on earth it was creation to unfold,
Spanning this mighty orb of ours as through the spheres it roll'd.
His name is written on the deep, the rivers as they run
Will bear it timeward o'er the world, telling what he hath done;
The story of his voyage to Death, amid the Arctic frosts,
Will be told by mourning mariners on earth's most distant coasts.

THE LAUNCH OF THE GRIFFIN

Within Cayuga's forest shade
The stocks were set—the keel was laid—
Wet with the nightly forest dew,
The frame of that first vessel grew.
Strange was the sight upon the brim
Of the swift river, even to him
   The builder of the bark;
To see its artificial lines
Festoon'd with summer's sudden vines,
   Another New World's ark.

As rounds to ripeness manhood's schemes
Out of youth's fond, disjointed dreams,
So ripen'd in her kindred wood
That traveller of the untried flood.
And often as the evening sun
Gleam'd on the group, their labor done—
   The Indian prowling out of sight
   Of corded friar and belted knight—
And smiled upon them as they smiled,
The builders on the bark—their child!

The hour has come: upon the stocks
The masted hull already rocks—
The mallet in the master's hand
Is poised to launch her from the land.
Beside him, partner of his quest
For the great river of the West,
Stands the adventurous *Recollet*
Whose page records that anxious day.
To him the master would defer
The final act—he will not bear
That any else than him who plann'd,
Should launch "the Griffin" from the land.
In courteous conflict they contend,

The knight and priest, as friend with friend—
    In that strange savage scene
The swift blue river glides before,
And still Niagara's awful roar
    Booms through the vistas green.

And now the mallet falls, stroke—stroke—
On prop of pine and wedge of oak
    The vessel feels her way;
The quick mechanics leap aside
As, rushing downward to the tide,
    She dashes them with spray.
The ready warp arrests her course,
And holds her for a while perforce,
While on her deck the merry crew
Man every rope, loose every clew,
    And spread her canvas free.
Away! 'tis done! the Griffin floats,
First of Lake Erie's winged boats—
    Her flag, the *Fleur-de-lis*.

Gun after gun proclaims the hour,
As nature yields to human power;
And now upon the deeper calm
The Indians hear the holy psalm—
Laudamus to the Lord of Hosts!
Whose name unknown on all their coasts,
The inmost wilderness shall know,
Wafted upon yon wings of snow
That, sinking in the waters blue,
Seem but some lake-bird lost to view.

In old romance and fairy lays
Its wondrous part the Griffin plays—
Grimly it guards the gloomy gate
Seal'd by the strong behest of Fate—
Or, spreading its portentous wings,
Wafts Virgil to the Court of Kings;
And unto scenes as wondrous shall
Thy Griffin bear thee, brave La Salle!
Thy winged steed shall stall where grows
On Michigan the sweet wild rose;
Lost in the mazes of St. Clair,
Shall give thee hope amid despair,
And bear thee past those isles of dread
The Huron peoples with the dead,
Where foot of savage never trod
Within the precinct of his god;
And it may be thy lot to trace
The footprints of the unknown race
'Graved on Superior's iron shore,
Which knows their very name no more.
Through scenes so vast and wondrous shall
Thy Griffin bear thee, brave La Salle—
True Wizard of the Wild! whose art,
An eye of power, a knightly heart,
A patient purpose silence-nursed,
A high, enduring, saintly trust—
Are mighty spells—we honor these,
Columbus of the inland seas!

"OUR LADYE OF THE SNOW!"

If, Pilgrim, chance thy steps should lead
Where, emblem of our holy creed,
      Canadian crosses glow—
There you may hear what here you read,
And seek, in witness of the deed,
      Our Ladye of the Snow!

In the old times when France held sway
From the Balize to Hudson's Bay
      O'er all the forest free,
A noble Breton cavalier
Had made his home for many a year
      Besides the Rivers Three.

To tempest and to trouble proof,
Rose in the wild his glitt'ring roof
      To every trav'ler dear;
The Breton song, the Breton dance,
The very atmosphere of France,
      Diffused a generous cheer.

Strange sight that on those fields of snow
The genial vine of Gaul should grow
      Despite the frigid sky!
Strange power of man's all-conqu'ring will,
That here the hearty Frank can still
      A Frenchman live and die!

The Seigneur's hair was ashen gray,
But his good heart held holiday,
      As when, in youthful pride,
He bared his shining blade before
De Tracey's regiment on the shore
      Which France has glorified.

Gay in the field, glad in the hall,
The first at danger's frontier call,
   The humblest devotee—
Of God and of St. Catherine dear
Was the stout Breton cavalier
   Beside the Rivers Three.

When bleak December's chilly blast
Fetter'd the flowing waters fast,
   And swept the frozen plain—
When, with a frighten'd cry, half heard,
Far southward fled the Arctic bird,
   Proclaiming winter's reign—

His custom was, come foul, come fair,
For Christmas duties to repair
   Unto the *Ville Marie*,
The city of the mount, which north
Of the great River looketh forth,
   Across its sylvan sea.

Fast fell the snow, and soft as sleep
The hillocks look'd like frozen sheep,
   Like giants gray the hills—
The sailing pine seem'd canvas-spread
With its white burden overhead,
   And marble hard the rills.

A thick dull light where ray was none
Of moon, or star, or cheerful sun,
   Obscurely show'd the way—
While merrily upon the blast
The jingling horse-bells, pattering fast,
   'Timed the glad roundelay.

Swift eve came on, and faster fell
The winnow'd storm on ridge and dell,
      Effacing shape and sign—
Until the scene grew blank at last,
As when some seaman from the mast
      Looks o'er the shoreless brine.

Nor marvel aught to find ere long
In such a scene the death of song
      Upon the bravest lips—
The empty only could be loud
When Nature fronts us in her shroud
      Beneath the sky's eclipse.

Nor marvel more to find the steed,
Though famed for spirit and for speed,
      Drag on a painful pace—
With drooping crest, and faltering foot,
And painful whine, the weary brute
      Seems conscious of disgrace.

Until he paused with mortal fear,
Then plaintive sank upon the mere
      Stiff as a steed of stone—
In vain the master winds his horn,
None, save the howling wolves forlorn
      Attend the dying roan.

Sad was the heart and sore the plight
Of the benumb'd, bewilder'd knight
      Now scrambling through the storm.
At every step he sank apace—
The death-dew freezing on his face—
      In vain each loud alarm!

The torpid echoes of the rock
Answer'd with one unearthly mock
      Of danger round about!
Then muffled in their snowy robes,
Retiring sought their bleak abodes,
      And gave no second shout.

Down on his knees himself he cast,
Deeming that hour to be his last,
      Yet mindful of his faith—
He pray'd St. Catherine and St. John,
And our dear Ladye call'd upon
      For grace of happy death.

When lo! a light beneath the trees,
Which clank their brilliants in the breeze—
      And lo! a phantom fair,
As God's in heaven! by that bless'd light
Our Lady's self rose to his sight
      In robes that spirits wear!

Oh! lovelier, lovelier far than pen,
Or tongue, or art, or fancy's ken
      Can picture, was her face—
Gone was the sorrow of the sword,
And the last passion of our Lord
      Had left no living trace!

As when the moon across the moor
Points the lost peasant to his door,
      And glistens on his pane—
Or when along her trail of light
Belated boatmen steer at night,
      A harbor to regain—

So the warm radiance from her hands
Unbind for him Death's icy bands,
    And nerve the sinking heart—
Her presence makes a perfect path.
Ah! he who such a helper hath
    May anywhere depart.

All trembling, as she onward smiled,
Follow'd that Knight our mother mild,
    Vowing a grateful vow—
Until far down the mountain gorge
She led him to the antique forge,
    Where her own shrine stands now.

If, Pilgrim, chance thy steps should lead
Where, emblem of our holy creed,
    Canadian crosses glow—
There you may hear what here you read,
And seek, in witness of the deed,
    Our Ladye of the Snow!

JACQUES CARTIER

In the seaport of Saint Malo, 'twas a smiling morn, in May,
When the Commodore Jacques Cartier to the westward sail'd
    away;
In the crowded old cathedral all the town were on their knees,
For the safe return of kinsmen from the undiscover'd seas;
And every autumn blast that swept o'er pinnacle and pier,
Fill'd manly hearts with sorrow and gentle hearts with fear.

A year pass'd o'er Saint Malo—again came round the day
When the Commodore Jacques Cartier to the westward sail'd
    away;
But no tidings from the absent had come the way they went,
And tearful were the vigils that many a maiden spent;
And manly hearts were fill'd with gloom, and gentle hearts with
    fear,
When no tidings came from Cartier at the closing of the year.

But the Earth is as the Future, it hath its hidden side,
And the Captain of Saint Malo was rejoicing, in his pride,
In the forests of the North—while his townsmen mourn'd his
    loss
He was rearing on Mount Royal the *fleur-de-lis* and cross;
And when two months were over and added to the year,
Saint Malo hail'd him home again, cheer answering to cheer.

He told them of a region, hard, iron-bound and cold,
Nor seas of pearl abounded, nor mines of shining gold,
Where the wind from Thulé freezes the word upon the lip,
And the ice in spring comes sailing athwart the early ship;
He told them of the frozen scene until they thrill'd with fear,
And piled fresh fuel on the hearth to make him better cheer.

But when he changed the strain—he told how soon is cast
In early spring the fetters that hold the waters fast;

How the winter causeway, broken, is drifted out to sea,
And the rills and rivers sing with pride the anthem of the free;
How the magic wand of summer clad the landscape, to his eyes,
Like the dry bones of the just, when they wake in Paradise.

He told them of the Algonquin braves—the hunters of the wild,
Of how the Indian mother in the forest rocks her child;
Of how, poor souls! they fancy, in every living thing
A spirit good or evil, that claims their worshipping;
Of how they brought their sick and maim'd for him to breathe upon,
And of the wonders wrought for them through the Gospel of St. John.

He told them of the river whose mighty current gave
Its freshness, for a hundred leagues, to Ocean's briny wave;
He told them of the glorious scene presented to his sight,
What time he rear'd the cross and crown on Hochelaga's height,
And of the fortress cliff that keeps of Canada the key,
And they welcomed back Jacques Cartier from his perils over sea.

JACQUES CARTIER AND THE CHILD

When Jacques Cartier return'd from his voyage to the westward,
All was uproar in Saint Malo and shouting of welcome—
Dear to his heart were the hail and the grasp of his townsmen,
And dear to his pride the favor and thanks of King Francis.
But of all who drew nigh—such was the cast of his nature—
A god-child beloved, he most delighted to answer
On all the surmises that fill the fancy of children.

"Tell me," she said, "what you found far away in the woodlands;
Say how you felt when you saw the savages standing
Arm'd on the shore, and heard the first sound of their war-cry?
Were you afraid then?" Quietly smiled the brave sailor—
"Nay, little daughter," he said, "I was not afraid of the red men;
But when I saw them, I sighed, alas! for the bondage,
The darkness that hangs over all the lost children of Adam.
As I in the depths of their forests might wander and wander
Deeper and deeper, and finding no outlet forever—
So they, in the old desolation of folly and error,
Are lost to their kindred divine in mansions eternal.

"And then, daughter dearest, I bless'd God in truth and in secret,
That he had not suffer'd my lot to be with the heathen,
But cast it in France—among a people so Christian;
And then I bethought me, peradventure to me it is given
To lead the vanguard of Truth to the inmost recesses
Of this lost region of souls who know not the Gospel.
And these were the thoughts I had far away in the woodlands,
When I saw the savages arm'd, and heard the roar of their
    war-cry."

THE ARCTIC INDIAN'S FAITH

We worship the Spirit that walks, unseen,
    Through our land of ice and snow:
We know not His face, we know not His place,
    But his presence and power we know.

Does the buffalo need the pale-face' word
    To find his pathway far?
What guide has he to the hidden ford,
    Or where the green pastures are?
Who teacheth the moose that the hunter's gun
    Is peering out of the shade?
Who teacheth the doe and the fawn to run
    In the track the moose has made?

Him do we follow, Him do we fear—
    The spirit of earth and sky;
Who hears with the *Wapiti's* eager ear
    His poor red children's cry.
Whose whisper we note in every breeze
    That stirs the birch canoe,
Who hangs the reindeer moss on the trees
    For the food of the *Caribou*.

That Spirit we worship who walks, unseen,
    Through our land of ice and snow:
We know not His face, we know not His place,
    But his presence and power we know.

PEACE HATH HER VICTORIES

To people wastes, to supplement the sun,
    To plant the olive where the wild-brier grew,
To bid rash rivers in safe channels run,
    The youth of aged cities to renew,
To shut the temple of the two-faced god—
    Grand triumphs these, worthy a conqueror's car;
They need no herald's horn, no lictor's rod;
    Peace hath her victories, no less than War.

To raise the drooping artist's head, to breathe
    The word despairing genius thirsts to hear,
To crown all service with its earned wreath,
    To be of lawless force the foe austere;
This is to stretch a sceptre over Time,
    This is to give our darkling earth a star,
And belt it with the emerald scroll sublime;
    Peace hath her victories, no less than War.

To stand amidst the passions of the hour
    Storm-lash'd, resounding fierce from shore to shore;
To watch the human whirlwind waste its power,
    Till drowned Reason lifts her head once more;
To build on hatred nothing; to be just,
    Judging of men and nations as they are,
Too strong to share the councils of mistrust;
    Peace hath her victories, no less than War.

To draw the nations in a silken bond,
    On to their highest exercise of good;
To show the better land above, beyond
    The sea of Egypt, all whose waves are blood;
These, leader of the age! these arts be thine,
    All vulgar victories surpassing far!
On these all heaven's benignant planets shine;
    Peace hath her victories, no less than War.

PARIS, April, 1867.

A PLEA FOR THE POOR

Sonnet

'Tis most true, madam! the poor wretch you turn'd
   Forth from your door was not of aspect fair;
His back was crooked, his eye, boa-like, burn'd,
   Wild and inhuman hung his matted hair;
His wit's unmannerly, uncouth his speech,
   Awkward his gait; but, madam, pray recall
How little Fate hath placed within his reach,
   His lot in life—that may account for all.
His bed hath been the inhospitable stones,
   His canopy the weeping mists of night;
Such savage shifts have warp'd his mind and bones,
   And sent him all unseemly to your sight.
Want is no courtier—Woe neglects all grace;
He hunger'd, and he had it in his face!

RICH AND POOR

A seasonable ditty

The rich man sat by his fire,
    Before him stood the wine,
He had all heart could desire,
    Save love of laws divine;
A daily growth of wealth,
    And the world's good word through all,
Wife, and children, and health,
    And clients in his hall.

The rich man walk'd about
    His large luxurious room,
His steps fell soft as the snows without,
    On the web of a Brussels loom;
Without, the bright icicles had
    Made lustres of all his trees,
And the garden gods look'd cold and sad
    In their snowy draperies.

The rich man look'd abroad
    Under the leaden sky,
And struggling up the gusty road,
    He saw a poor man go by;
He paused and lean'd on the gate,
    To husband his scanty breath,
Then feebly down on the threshold sate,
    The counterfeit of death!

The rich man turn'd his head
    And close his curtains drew,
And by his warm hearth, gleaming red,
    The wine-fledg'd hours fast flew;
Without, on the cold, cold stone,
    The poor man's head reclined,
A snow-quilt over him blown,
    A body without a mind!

The rich man's sleep that night
    Was vinous, dreamy, and deep,
Till near the dawn, when a spectre white
    He saw, and heard it weep;
He rose, and stepping forth,
    Beheld a sight of woe—
His brother Abel on the earth
    Slain and hid in the snow!

The stone received the head
    Rejected by the brother;
'Twas of colder cause he lay there dead
    Than the cold of the winter weather!
His blue lips gaped apart,
    And the snow that lapp'd his frame,
Lay through life on the rich man's heart
    After that night of shame.

FALSE FEAR OF THE WORLD

An impromptu

"The World!" "The World! why, plague it, man,
 Why do you shake your world at me?
For all its years, and all your fear,
 The thing I am I still must be.
I see! I see! fine homes on hills,
 With winding pathways smooth and fair;
But let me moil among the mills,
 Rather than creep to riches there.

"A heather bell on Travail's cliffs,
 Smells sweeter than a garden rose;
The lumber-barge outsails the skiffs,
 And saves men's lives when Boreas blows.
'Tis, sure, enough to note the day,
 With morning hail, and night adieu,
Nor squander precious hours away
 With Affectation's empty crew.

"My friend's my friend, my foe's my foe;
 I have my hours of joy and gloom;
I do not love all mankind—No!
 The heart I have has not the room.
But there is half-a-score I know,
 And her, and you, and this wee thing,
Who make my World, my all, below—
 Cause, Constitution, Country, King!"

GRANDMA ALICE

I had just now a curious dream.
    While dozing after dinner,
I dreamt I saw above my bed
    (As sure as I'm a sinner)—
In words and figures broad and tall,
    With flourishes a-plenty,
"This is the time that mortals call
    The year Nineteen Hundred Twenty!"

I rubb'd my eyes—in fancy rubb'd—
    To find myself beholder
Of any date so ancient dubb'd
    And sixty summers older.
I look'd about,—'twas Cornwall town,
    But grown as fine as Florence!
Only the river rolling down
    Look'd like the old St. Lawrence.

Out from a shady garden green
    Came ringing shouts of laughter,
I watch'd the chase, myself unseen,
    The flight, and running after;
A group of matronly mamas,
    With scions in abundance,
Who pour'd around their pleased papas
Their spirits' wild redundance.

Hard by a thickly-blooming bower,
    Rosy, and close, and shady,
I saw, beguiling eve's calm hour,
    A venerable lady:
Her eyes were on a well-worn book,
    And, as she turn'd the pages,
There was that meaning in her look
    Which sculptors give to sages.

Sometimes she smiled and sometimes sigh'd,
   As leaf by leaf she ponder'd;
Sometimes there was a touch of pride,
   Sometimes she paused and wonder'd;
Her station seem'd all plain to me—
   A grand-dame hale and hearty—
Happy and proud was she to see
   The gambols of the party.

I closer drew, and well I knew,
   In Nineteen Hundred Twenty,
The lady's book was old, not new—
   I caught a well-known entry!
The lady's years of life had pass'd
   Unsour'd by care or malice;
The book—this album 'twas, she clasped—
   They call'd her GRAND-MA ALICE!

CORNWALL, C.W., 1861

"This playful *jeu d'esprit* was written in the album of a very young lady in 1861." [*T.D.M.*]

AUTUMN AND WINTER

An antique

Autumn, the squire of Winter, is abroad,
Making much dust upon the breezy road;
His Joseph coat with every hue is gay,
But seems as if't had known a sunnier day;
His master from the North is drawing nigh,
Fur-clad, and little favor'd to mine eye.

And yet this piebald courier doth him wrong;
He loves a friend, a bottle, and a song;
His memory's a mine, whereof the ore
Is ever-wrought and never-ending lore.
His white locks hide a head full of rare dreams,
Which by a friendly fire with gladness streams,
While Christmas shrives the perishing Old year
He leads the New out from behind the bier.

Oh! motley Autumn, prithee mend thy pace,
I do not like thy costume nor thy face;
Thy hollow laugh and stage proprieties
Tell of a bungling actor, ill at ease,—
To live such life as thine is shame, is sin;
Prithee fall back, let honest Winter in.

THE MOUNTAIN-LAUREL

Far upon the sunny mountain, laurel groves were growing,
Silently adown the river came a hot youth, rowing;
      Looking up, afar he spied
      The green groves on the mountain side—
      Quoth the youth, and fondly sigh'd,—
"I'll pluck your plumes, and sail anon, fair the wind is blowing!"

Landing, then, he took his way to where the groves were growing;
Far he travell'd, all the morn, from the calm stream flowing;
      In the sultry June noontide,
      He reach'd the groves he had espied,
      And sat down on the mountain side;
"Sing the snowy, plumy laurels, laurels gaily blowing!"

Sat and slept within the groves of laurels bright and blowing,
Oh! the deadly laurel-tree, with flowering poison glowing!
      Down they fell on lip and brain,
      Oh! that odorous, deadly rain!
      He never shall return again
To his boat, upon the stream afar, so calm and gently flowing!

THE DEATH-BED

Up amid the Ulster mountains,
    Oh, my brother!
Where the heath-bells fringe the fountains,
    Oh, my brother!
Like a light through darkness beaming,
Like a well, in deserts streaming—
Like relief in dismal dreaming,
    I beheld her, oh, my brother!

Hair like midnight, eyes like morning,
    Oh, my brother!
Breaking on me without warning,
    Oh, my brother!
Shooting forth fire so resistless,
That my heart is low and listless,
And my eyes of Earth are wistless,
    Oh, my brother!

Daily, nightly, I've been pining,
    Oh, my brother!
For those eyes like morning shining,
    Oh, my brother!
And that voice! like music sighing
O'er the beds of minstrels dying,
'Twas a voice there is no flying,
    Oh, my brother!

Say not, hope—oh! rather listen,
    Oh, my brother!
When the evening dew-drops glisten,
    Oh, my brother!
On the grass above me growing,
Strew my grave with blossoms blowing,
Where that haunted fount is flowing,
    Oh, my brother!

Where her feet did print the heather,
    Oh, my brother!
Grace and goodness grow together,
    Oh, my brother!
Even yon wither'd wreath doth move me,
Seems to say, she might have loved me—
Strew no other flowers above me,
    Oh, my brother!

DARK BLUE EYES

Strange that Nature's loveliness,
Should conceal destructiveness;
Pestilence in Indian bowers,
Serpents 'mid Italian flowers,
Stranger still the woe that lies
In a pair of dark blue eyes!

In my dreams they hover o'er me,
In my walks they go before me,
Read I cannot while there dances
O'er the page, one of those glances;
Musing upward on the skies
There I find those dark blue eyes!

Woe is me! those orbs of ether
Can I win, or banish, neither!
Never to be mine, and never
To be banish'd by endeavor;
Still my peace delusive flies
Before those haunting dark blue eyes!

A CONTRAST

Imitated from the Irish

Bebinn is straight as a poplar,
   Queenly and comely to see,
But she seems so fit for a sceptre,
   She never could give it to me.
Aine is lithe as a willow,
   And her eye, whether tearful or gay,
So true to her thought, that in Aine
   I find a new charm every day.

Bebinn calmly and silently sails
   Down life's stream like a snow-breasted swan;
She's so lonesomely grand, that she seems
   To shrink from the presence of man.
Aine basks in the glad summer sun,
   Like a young dove let loose in the air;
Sings, dances, and laughs—but for me
   Her joy does not make her less fair.

Oh! give me the nature that shows
   Its emotions of mirth or of pain,
As the water that glides, and the corn that grows,
   Show shadow and sunlight again.
Oh! give me the brow that can bend,
   Oh! give me the eyes that can weep,
And give me a heart like Lough Neagh,
   As full of emotions and deep.

TO MARY'S ANGEL

A Valentine

Ye angels, to whom space is not,
    Who span the earth like light,
Keep watch and ward around the spot
    Where dwells my heart's delight;
And when my true love walks abroad,
    Spread roses in her path,
And let the winds, round her abode,
    Subdue their wail and wrath.

Ye angels, ye were made to be
    To one another kind;
And she to whom I charge ye, see,
    Your sister is in mind;
As gentle as soft strains, as wild
    As zephyrs in their youth,
As artless as a country child,
    The very word of truth.

Ye guard the sailor far at sea,
    The hermit in his cell;
Yet they are less alone than she—
    Good angels, watch her well!
He who should be her guard and guide,
    Alas! is far away;
Ye spirits, leave not Mary's side,
    I charge ye, night or day!

CONSOLATION

Men seek for treasure in the earth;
   Where I have buried mine,
There never mortal eye shall pierce,
   Nor star nor lamp shall shine!
We know, my love, oh! well we know,
   The secret treasure-spot,
Yet must our tears forever fall,
   Because that *they* are not.

How gladly would we give to light
   The ivory forehead fair—
The eye of heavenly-beaming blue,
   The clust'ring chestnut hair—
Yet look around this mournful scene
   Of daily earthly life,
And could you wish them back to share
   Its sorrow and its strife?

If blessèd angels stray to earth,
   And seek in vain a shrine,
They needs must back return again
   Unto their source divine:
All life obeys the unchanging law
   Of him who took and gave,
We count a glorious saint in heaven
   For each child in the grave.

Look up, my love, look up, afar,
   And dry each bitter tear,
Behold three white-robed innocents
   At heaven's high gate appear!
For you and me and those we love,
   They smilingly await—
God grant we may be fit to join
   Those Angels of the Gate.

A SMALL CATECHISM

Why are children's eyes so bright?
    Tell me why?
'Tis because the infinite
Which they've left, is still in sight,
And they know no earthly blight—
    Therefore 'tis their eyes are bright.

Why do children laught so gay?
    Tell me why?
'Tis because their hearts have play
In their bosoms, every day,
Free from sin and sorrow's sway—
    Therefore 'tis they laugh so gay.

Why do children speak so free?
    Tell me why?
'Tis because from fallacy,
Cant, and seeming, they are free,
Hearts, not lips, their organs be—
    Therefore 'tis they speak so free.

Why do children love so true?
    Tell me why?
'Tis because they cleave unto
A familiar, favorite few,
Without art or self in view—
    Therefore children love so true.

GOD BE PRAISED!

I am young and I love labor,
    God be praised!
I have many a kindly neighbor,
    God be praised!
I've a wife—my whole love bought her,
And a little prattling daughter,
With eyes blue as ocean water,
    God be praised!

Care or guilt have not deform'd me,
    God be praised!
Tasks and trials but inform'd me,
    God be praised!
I have been no base self-seeker;
With the mildest I am meeker;
I have made no brother weaker,
    God be praised!

I have dreamt youth's dreams elysian,
    God be praised!
And for many an unreal vision
    God be praised!
But of manhood's lessons sterner
Long I've been a patient learner,
And now wear with ease life's armor,
    God be praised!

The world is not all evil,
    God be praised!
It must amend if we will,
    God be praised!
Healing vervain oft we find

With fell hemlock intertwined;
Hate, not Love, was born blind,
    God be praised!

Calm night to day is neighbor,
    God be praised!
So rest succeeds to labor,
    God be praised!
By deeds, not days, lives number,
Time's conquerors still slumber,
Their own master-pieces under,
    God be praised!

CHRISTMAS MORN

Up, Christian! hark! the crowing cock
   Proclaims the break of day!
Up! light the lamp, undo the lock,
   And take the well-known way.
Already through the painted glass
Streams forth the light of early Mass!

Our altar! oh, how fair it shows
   Unto the night-dimm'd eyes!
Oh! surely yonder leaf that glows,
   Was pluck'd in Paradise!
Without, it snows; the wind is loud;
Earth sleeps, wrapp'd in her yearly shroud.

Within, the organ's soaring peal,
   The choir's sweet chant, the bells,
The surging crowd that stands or kneels,
   The glorious errand tells.
Rejoice! rejoice! ye sons of men,
For man may hope for heaven again!

'Tis but a step, a threshold cross'd,
   Yet such a change we find;
Without, the wand'ring worldling toss'd
   By every gust of wind;
Within, there reigns a holy calm,
For here abides the dread "I AM"!

THE MIDNIGHT MASS

Where the mountains gray and weary,
    Watch above the valley pass,
Come the frieze-clad upland people,
    To the Midnight Mass;
Where the red stream rushes hoarsely
    Through the bridge o'ergrown with grass,
Come the whispering troops of neighbors,
    To the Midnight Mass!

No moon walks heaven's high hall as mistress,
    No stars pierce the drifting rocks,
Only wind-gusts try back, whining
    Like dogs on a dubious track.
Hark! there comes a startling echo
    Upward through the central arch!
'Tis the swollen flood that carries,
    Captive off, a raft of larch.

Shines a light; it is the Chapel—
    Softly, 'tis the hour of God;
Poor and small, yet far more lowly
    Was the infant Christ's abode;
Rude and stoney is the pavement,
    Plain and bare the altar-stone;
Ruder was the crib of Bethlehem
    Over which the east star shone.

Confiteor! God of ages,
    Mercy's everlasting source!
I have sinned, oh! do Thou give me
    Strength to stem my passion's force!
Mea culpa! mea culpa!
    Saviour of the world and me,
By thy Passion, oh! have mercy,
    Thorn-crown'd of Calvary!

Gloria in excelsis Deo!
    Shout the pæan to the sky!
Eyes of faith, in yon poor stable,
    See disguised Divinity.
Gloria in excelsis Deo!
    Christ, the hope of man, is born!
Shout the anthem! join the angels!
    'Tis our Saviour's natal morn.

Praise to God, the Eternal Father,
    Who of clay created man!
Praise to Christ, who trod the wine-press
    Till the atonement overran!
Praise to Him, the Holy Spirit,
    Who inform'd our souls with grace!
Alleluia! 'tis the morning
    Of redemption for our race!

LIFE, A MYSTERY TO MAN

You ask me, comrade, "why I speak with awe,
Harping forever on this Theme of Life,
As if it were the only care of man,
Instead of being a rope of slipp'ry strands,
Full of vile accidents, vexations, dreams;
A taper made but to be burnèd out,
A better sort of shroud, a thistle-down,
The airy carriage of an unsown seed,
The wooden shedding of a lasting structure,
A very flimsy, miserable makeshift,
Neither an art, nor yet a mystery?"

Life *is* a mystery, *might* be an art!
Old men know all its secret sleights and laws,
But when they learn to live, 'tis time to die,
And so their knowledge, age by age, goes with them;
And the young still begin to live, as though
A past were not, and future could not be.

It is Life's noon, and the young soul looks out:
Oh Earth! how fond and beautiful thou art!
How blue the sky is! How benign the sun!
How glorified the night! How joyous Spring
And all the seasons look! He's told
"Life's but a voyage, a river, and a dream;"
And this he takes as literal, nor thinks
The voyager's port is death; the river's end
Is in the sea, eternity; the dream once over,
The sleeper wakes up face to face with God!
He comprehends life's sacred sense no more
Than the mute trumpet does the word it utters.

Upward he goes, a-gathering shells and toys,
As if God sent him museum-making; or,

Sitting at some siren's feet of clay,
He sings away the hours with wanton airs,
Flinging his reason from him: then for days
He will be searching after it, that he
May squander it once more.
He's heard that amid roses beautiful,
Remorse, even as crocodiles of Nile,
Chooseth his den; he well knows that a poison,
Deadliest to men, has ever been distilled
From the fair blossoms of the laurel tree;
Yet, like some laughing child of Memphis old,
Playing among the sphinxes, never notes
That Good and Evil, from their dateless posts
Regard him with their all-unwearied eyes;
He never thinks, while looking at his watch,
A spirit sits within the works to note
His actions by the hour; he little dreams,
Sleep-walker as he is, that even now
Angels descend from heaven every day,
And might be seen if we had Jacob's grace.
His lawless will he makes his only law,
His god is pleasure, and his devil, pain.

   The first great end of life, is to be saved;
And next, to leave the world the better for us.
Both are commanded, both are possible.
No good man's life was ever lived in vain:
Like hidden springs they freshen all around,
And by the lonely verdure of their sphere,
You know where good men dwelt.

But man's true empire is his deathless soul—
How capable of culture and adornment!
His memory, which, from the distant years,
Drives its long camel-cavalcades of lore;
His will, a curb'd steed or a cataract,
Full of directness, loftiness and power,
If it were rightly schooled; his reason,
An armory of Archimedean levers,
Such as, reposing on the Word of God,
Might raise the world! Will man never know
To rule the empire in himself contained,
Its hosts of passions, tastes, affections, hopes;
Each one a priceless blessing to its lord,
If subject to Religion's holy law?

Ah! were there many rulers among men,
How fragrant in God's nostrils would become
This reeling, riotous, and rotten earth!
Then should we see no more guilt and remorse,
Life's vernal and autumnal equinox,
Shaking down roof-trees on defenceless heads,
Scattering the fairest hopes of dearest friends,
And strewing peaceful places with the wreck
Of lofty expectation; then premature old age,
And gray hairs without honor, could not be;
Nor orphans rankly cumbering the waste,
Like garden-seeds to some far prairie blown;
Then blessed peals would daily fill the air,
And God's house be familiar as our own;
Then Faith, and Truth, and patient Charity,
Returning from their long sojourn in heaven,
With all their glorious arts and gentle kin,
Would colonize this moral wilderness,
Making it something like what God design'd!

Thus would I have my friend consider life,
And, like the diver in the secret sea,
Open his eyes and see it all reveal'd—
Quicksands, currents, monsters, weeds, and shoals.
Thus would I have him school, in humbleness,
His ear to catch the rhythmic admonitions
Which come, upon the wings of every wind,
From the far shore where the dead ages dwell.
I would have him entertain such thoughts,
That, being with him, they might still preserve
His feet from pitfalls, and his cheek from shame,
His heart from sorrow, and his soul from woe.

ACKNOWLEDGEMENT

D'Arcy McGee has been well served by his biographers, and I have relied a great deal upon their researches.

The original, candid and exhaustive 1925 biography, *The Life of Thomas D'Arcy McGee* by Isabel Skelton, is the definitive work.

Alexander Brady's *Thomas D'Arcy McGee*, published the same year, is a much shorter book (in the Macmillan *Canadian Statesman* series) but is reliable, urbane and an excellent introduction.

My personal favourite, and my guide through this project, has been Josephine Phelan's *The Ardent Exile*, published in 1951. It is humblingly well-written.

For readers whose primary interest in McGee is Irish and political, *The Assassination of Thomas D'Arcy McGee* by Patrick Phelan is indispensible.